Al Smith

Radio

T0347918

methuen | drama

LONDON • NEW YORK • OXFORD • NEW DELHI • SYDNEY

METHUEN DRAMA
Bloomsbury Publishing Plc
50 Bedford Square. London WC1B 3DP. UK
1385 Broadway, New York, NY 10018, USA

BLOOMSBURY, METHUEN DRAMA and the Methuen Drama logo
are trade marks of Bloomsbury Publishing Plc

First published as an original audio book by Audible in 2019

Cover design: Ben Anslow
Artwork © James Jackson / Voikukka
Photography © Simon Annand

A catalogue record for this book is available from the British Library.
A catalog record for this book is available from the Library of Congress.

ISBN: PB: 978-1-3501-3838-4
ePDF: 978-1-3501-3839-1
eBook: 978-1-3501-3840-7

Series: Modern Plays

Typeset by Country Setting, Kingdown, Kent CT14 8ES

To find out more about our authors and books visit www.bloomsbury.com
and sign up for our newsletters.

RADIO
By Al Smith

This version was first produced by Audible at the Arcola Theatre
on 19th June - 13th July 2019

Original production dates

Radio was first produced by Kandinsky for the Edinburgh Festival Fringe in August 2006. It
transferred to the Brits Off Broadway Festival at 59E59 Theaters New York in June 2007.

The characters in this play are fictional. Any similarity to persons living or dead is entirely
coincidental and not intentional.

Please note that the text of the play which appears in this volume may be changed during the
rehearsal process and appear in a slightly altered form in performance.

There will be no interval.

Running time approximately 1 hr 15 mins.

Politics in America since 2016 has been maddeningly addictive. Watching a country wrestle with a demon of its own creation is an extraordinary spectacle. Of course we Brits are, rather obviously, not immune to this phenomenon either.

I feel like we're watching America's greatest assets pollinate the country's greatest weaknesses – faith in enterprise promoting faith in wealth, national pride fertilising xenophobia, optimism becoming delusion.

And this isn't anything new – here we are 50 years on from Apollo 11, America's greatest moment of paradox. 1968 saw new political coalitions led by Bobby Kennedy and Martin Luther King, and yet also bore witness to the My Lai massacre in Vietnam, where American boys killed five hundred Vietnamese civilians. 1969 saw Neil Armstrong landing on the moon, and Richard Nixon landing in the White House.

Was the Apollo programme any different? After all, NASA had two missions: to explore space for the good of mankind, and to make absolutely sure the Russians didn't do it first.

Al Smith is a unique writer, able to arrange four or five thematic conversations alongside each other in one piece of work. Radio is no exception, exploring the contradictions at the heart of the USA without ducking any of the complexity. Placing his script in the hands of an actor like Adam Gillen has made my job very simple. I have been mostly trying to stay out of the way.

JOSH ROCHE - Director

audible

Audible is a rich listening destination that offers insight and inspiration to millions of listeners and is the world's leading audio and spoken-word media service. Audible's theatre initiative unleashes the artistic creativity of playwrights around the globe to deliver language-driven storytelling and inspire captivating performances on stage and in audio. In the UK, Audible co-produced Julia Leigh's critically acclaimed play, Avalanche starring Maxine Peake and the Fringe First winning production of On the Exhale by Martin Zimmerman in Edinburgh. In New York, Audible's productions include Harry Clarke by David Cale starring Billy Crudup, Girls & Boys by Dennis Kelly starring Carey Mulligan and Patti Smith: Words and Music. In audio, Audible has produced Iphigenia in Splott by Gary Owen starring Sophie Melville, True West starring Kit Harington and Johnny Flynn, The Diary of a Hounslow Girl written and starring Ambreen Razia and more. In 2017, Audible launched a five million-dollar Emerging Playwrights Fund that identifies, nurtures and invests in emerging playwrights, making their works available to millions of listeners around the world.

AUDIBLE STAFF

Founder & CEO – Don Katz
EVP & Publisher – Beth Anderson
SVP Content & Publishing EU - Michael Treutler
Chief Financial Officer – Cynthia Chu
SVP, Country Manager, UK - Tracey Markham
Head of Legal – Stas Zakharenko

Theatre
Artistic Producer – Kate Navin
Commissioning Producer, UK – Abigail Gonda
Producer, Music Initiative – Preston Copley
Producer, New Play Development and Commissions – Emilia LaPenta
Producer, Theatre and Original Content – Franki de La Vega

Studios
Director, Audible Studios UK – Katie Arlett
Production Manager – David Darlington
Casting and Talent Manager – Mariele Runacre-Temple
Casting and Production Manager – Nicola Wall
Production Co-ordinator – Yuki Parmar

Business Affairs
Audible Originals, Theatre – Jessica Amato
Manager – Alexandra Hargreaves

Legal
Senior Corporate Counsel – Nick Glynn
Corporate Counsel – Katherine Teasdale

Finance
Senior Director, Finance – Clare Jarvis
Financial Controller – Rich Talbot

Press
Director of Communications – Richard Noble
Communications Manager – Tom Curry

Marketing
Director, UK Brand Marketing - Matthew Parker
Content Marketing Manager – Bryony Cullen
UK Editorial Merchandising Manager – Frances Earlam

arcola
theatre

Arcola produces daring, high-quality theatre in the heart of East London and beyond.

We commission and premiere exciting, original works alongside rare gems of world drama and bold new productions of classics.

Our socially-engaged, international programme champions diversity, challenges the status quo, and attracts over 65,000 people to our building each year. Ticket prices are some of the most affordable in London, and our long-running Pay What You Can scheme ensures there is no financial barrier to accessing the theatre.

Every year, we offer 26 weeks of free rehearsal space to BAME and refugee artists; our Grimeborn Festival opens up opera with contemporary stagings at affordable prices; and our Participation department creates over 13,500 creative opportunities for the people of Hackney and beyond. Our pioneering environmental initiatives are award-winning, and aim to make Arcola the world's first carbon-neutral theatre.

Game Changers
Graham and Christine Benson, Roger Bradburn & Helen Main, Andrew Cripps, Robert Fowler, Daniel Friel, David Alan & Jean Grier, Sarah Morrison, Rosie Schumm

Trailblazers
Katie Bradford, Catrin Evans, Gold Family, Jon Gilmartin, Stuart Honey, Melanie Johnson, Katrin Maeurich

---

www.arcolatheatre.com   020 7503 1646

Artistic Director
Mehmet Ergen

Executive Producer
Leyla Nazli

Executive Director
Ben Todd

Associate Director
Jack Gamble

Producer
Richard Speir

New Work Assistant
Eleanor Dawson

Finance & Operations

Operations Manager
Natalja Derendiajeva

Finance Manager
Steve Haygreen

Finance Assistant
Marcela Royas

IT Manager and Software Developer
Nick Cripps

IT Assistant and Software Developer
Oliver Brill

Health and Safety Manager
Charlotte Croft

Health and Safety Assistant
Miriam Mahony

Sustainability Assistant
Helen Freudenberg

Participation

Participation Manager
Bec Martin-Williams

Participation Coordinator
Rach Skyer

Production

Head of Production
Geoff Hense

Chief Technician
Michael Paget

Front of House

Front of House & Box Office Manager
Norna Yau

Front of House & Box Office
Assistant Manager &
Access Development Manager
James York

Front of House Supervisors
Emily Jones, Mary Roubos

Cleaner
Suber Kemal Sabit

Arcola Bar

Bar Events Manager
Shanker Krishnan

MAKE THIS HAPPEN

Text **ARCO14 £3** to 70070
to give £3 in support of Arcola

Standard network charges apply.

ADAM GILLEN – Charlie Fairbanks

Since graduating from RADA in 2007, Adam has worked extensively on stage and screen. 2019 gained Adam an Olivier nomination for his performance in Killer Joe (Trafalgar Studios) for best supporting actor, prior to which he garnered great reviews for his role as Mozart in Peter Shaffer's Amadeus (National Theatre). Other theatre includes Martin in Wendy and Peter (RSC), School for Scandal (Barbican), The Door Never Closes (Almeida), For King and Country (Plymouth Theatre Royal), A Taste of Honey (Royal Exchange Theatre) which he was nominated for a TMA Award for Best Supporting Performance for his role as Geoffrey. Proper Clever (Liverpool Playhouse); The Good Soul of Szechuan (Young Vic); The Lion's Mouth and War and Peace (Royal Court); The Five Wives of Maurice Pinder (National Theatre).

On screen Adam is perhaps best known as Brian in award-winning Fresh Meat (Objective Productions/C4) and as Liam in Benidorm (Tiger Aspect/ITV). Adam's other screen credits include Vita and Virginia (Mirror Films); Miss Wright (ITV); Prisoner's Wives (Tiger Aspect/BBC); This is Jinsy (Sky Atlantic; Funny Cow (Gizmo Films); Set Fire to The Stars (Mad as Birds); We Are The Freaks (104 Film); 4,3,2,1 (Unstoppable Entertainment).

Writer	Al Smith
Director	Josh Roche
Designer	Sophie Thomas
Lighting Designer	Peter Small
Sound Designer	Ella Wahlström
Producer	Abigail Gonda for Audible
Production Manager	Ian Taylor
Assistant Director	Kaleya Baxe
Stage Manager	Megan Bly
Dialect Coach	Martin McKellan

General Management - Paul Casey and Julia Nye for
Arden Entertainment
www.arden-entertainment.co.uk

Kate Morley and Freya Cowdry for
Kate Morley PR
www.katemorleypr.com

Marketing by Boom Ents

www.Boom-Ents.com

With thanks to:

Angels, Production Cover Artwork by Photographer Simon Annand, all the staff and
management of Arcola Theatre, Iain Armstrong and team at Iain Armstrong Pictures,
Bloomsbury Publishing, Collins & Company, Integro Insurance, London Welsh Centre, Rosie
Murray, PRS, Marco Savo, White Light

AL SMITH – Writer

Al was a Pearson Playwright in Residence at the Finborough Theatre, was attached to Paines Plough's Future Perfect Scheme and graduated from the BBC Writers Academy. In 2012 Al won the BFI Wellcome Trust Screenwriting Prize. In 2017 his radio series Life Lines won gold for Best Fictional Storytelling at the ARIAS, the Radio Academy Awards and Best Series at the Audio Drama Awards, and he was nominated for the Charles Wintour Award for Most Promising Playwright at the 2017 for his play Harrogate.

Theatre: Harrogate (HighTide Festival, Royal Court); Diary of a Madman (Traverse Theatre, Gate Theatre); Sport (Finborough Theatre); The Bird (Underbelly, Arcola); The Astronaut Wives Club (Soho Theatre); Radio (Underbelly, 59E59 NYC); Enola (Underbelly, Arches).

Radio: First Do No Harm (BBC Radio 4); Life Lines (Two Series for BBC Radio 4); Culture (BBC Radio 4); Everyman (Co-written for BBC Radio 3); Duchamp's Urinal (Co-written for BBC Radio 4); Everyday Time Machines (BBC Radio 3); Life in the Freezer (BBC Radio 4); The Postman of Good Hope (BBC Radio 4); Radio (BBC Radio 4); Ok Computer (Co-written for BBC Radio 4).

Television: EastEnders (BBC); Father Brown (BBC); Shakespeare Live (BBC/RSC); The Coroner (BBC); Africa (BBC/Discovery); The Cut (BBC).

JOSH ROCHE – Director

Josh Roche is the winner of the JMK Award 2017, directing My Name is Rachel Corrie at the Young Vic. Other theatre credits include Orlando, This Must Be The Place (VAULT Festival); Plastic (Old Red Lion/ Mercury Theatre); Magnificence, A Third (Finborough Theatre); I Feel Fine, Specie, Uninvited (New Diorama Theatre). Previously he was Writer's Centre Associate at the Soho Theatre, and Artistic Director of Fat Git Theatre. He is currently an Associate Reader for Sonia Friedman Productions, and Associate Director with Poleroid Theatre. He has worked as an assistant director with John Dove, Gregory Doran, Polly Findlay, Maria Aberg, Joe Murphy and Steve Marmion and has directed one-off events for Shakespeare's Globe and the Royal Shakespeare Company.

SOPHIE THOMAS – Designer

Sophie Thomas is a Bristol based Set & Costume Designer for theatre film and live events. Recent design credits include Costume Design for Carnage: Swallowing the Past by Simon Amstell, available on BBC iPlayer. Theatre credits include: My Name Is Rachel Corrie (Young Vic), Orlando (Vaults Festival), Plastic (Old Red Lion), The Slave (Tristan Bates), Henry V (Cambridge Arts Theatre). Film credits include: The Listener (BAFTA Long List for Best Short Film), New Gods (New York Film Festival), Never Land (BFI Futures Festival). Sophie designed BAS' Too High To Riot US Tour in 2017. That same year Sophie was invited to talk at The Do Lectures, Wales.

Sophie was Resident Trainee Designer at the Royal Shakespeare Company 2015-16. Productions included: Love to Love, King Lear, The Alchemist, Dream 16, Dr. Faustus, Cymbeline and Hamlet. Sophie has assisted international and national designers including Tom Scutt, Tom Piper, Stephen Brimson-Lewis, Naomi Dawson, Niki Turner, Helen Goddard and Anna Fleischle.

PETER SMALL - Lighting Designer

Peter is an Offie and Theatre & Technology Award nominated lighting designer working across theatre, dance and opera.

Recent lighting designs for theatre include Square Go (59E59 Theaters, New York and Roundabout); Angry Alan (Soho Theatre); Ad Libido (VAULT Festival, Edinburgh Fringe and Soho Theatre); YOU STUPID DARKNESS! (Theatre Royal Plymouth); How to Spot an Alien, Sticks and Stones and Island Town (Paines Plough Roundabout); Out of Love, Black Mountain (Offie Nominated) and How To Be A Kid (Roundabout and Orange Tree); Orlando (VAULT); Plastic (Poleroid Theatre, Old Red Lion); Old Fools (Southwark Playhouse); A Girl In School Uniform (walks into a bar) (Offie and Theatre & Technology Award Nominated - New Diorama); She Called Me Mother (Pitch Lake Productions, UK Tour); East End Boys and West End Girls (Arcola Theatre, UK tour); A Midsummer Night's Dream, Free Association and Crazy Lady (Forum Alpbach, Austria); Richard III and Bard on Board 2 (Queen Mary 2 Ocean Liner).

Lighting for Opera and Musicals include The Rape of Lucretia (Stratford Circus); All or Nothing (West End, and tour); Cinderella (Loughborough Theatre); Tom & Jerry (EventBox Theatre, Egypt); The Venus Factor (Bridewell Theatre). Revival Lighting Designer on Kiss Me Kate for Oper Graz.

ELLA WAHLSTRÖM - Sound Designer

Ella Wahlström is an international Sound Designer. She was born in Finland and moved to London in 2010 to train at Rose Bruford College. Her latest sound design is for Jellyfish which plays at The National Theatre and tours the UK 2019. She's the sound designer of Esa-Pekka Salonen's Cello Concerto which premiered in Chicago in 2017 with Yo-Yo Ma as the soloist and the co-sound designer of Robert Wilson and Mikhail Baryshnikov's Letter to a Man. Other Sound Design credits include: Peter Pan Goes Wrong (London West End, UK and international tour), Black&White (SJACC, Kuwait), Trying it On (UK tour, RSC, Royal Court), Inside Bitch (Royal Court).

IAN TAYLOR - Production Manager

Trained at Guildhall School of Music and Drama. Founded by Ian in 2014, eStage provides theatre and event production services for the entertainment industry through a network of experienced production managers, builders, artists and technicians. Theatre includes Cash Cow and Wilderness (Hampstead Theatre), The Sweet Science of Bruising and Dear Brutus (Southwark Playhouse) and Rasheeda Speaking (Trafalgar Studios) for Troupe. Other People's Money, The Funeral Director, Trestle, Diary of a Teenage Girl, Orca and Tomcat (Southwark Playhouse), Robin Hood (The Bussey Building), Keith?,

Stop and Search, New Nigerians, The Plague, Not Talking, The Blue Hour of Natalie Barney, Thebes Land, The Cherry Orchard, The Lower Depths, After Independence, The Island Nation, Werther, Pelléas et Mélisande and Il Tabarro (Arcola Theatre), Reflected (Platform Southwark), Schism (Park Theatre), Giulio Cesare and Così fan tutte (Bury Court Opera), Hanna (Arcola Theatre and National Tour), The Cutlass Crew, The Price, Deep Waters, The Fizz and Eliza and the Swans (W11 Opera), L'Agrippina (The Barber Institute of Fine Arts, University of Birmingham), Our House (National Tour), Whisper House (The Other Palace), Oedipus Rex and L'Enfant et Les Sortilèges (The Philharmonia Orchestra at Royal Festival Hall), The Man Who Would Be King, Peter Pan and Red Riding Hood (Greenwich Theatre), Vanities: The Musical (Trafalgar Studios), Who Framed Roger Rabbit? (Future Cinema)

MEGAN BLY - Stage Manager

Megan Bly trained at LAMDA (FdA - Stage Management and Technical Theatre).

Credits Include: Miss Nightingale (Mister Bugg Presents), Carmen – The Gypsy (Romany Theatre Company), Don Pasquale (Wexford Festival Opera), Partenope and La Boheme (Iford Arts), L'incoronazione di Poppea (Trinity Laban), La Boheme (Clonter Opera), Don Giovanni (Opera Loki), English Eccentrics (British Youth Opera), Tumulus by Christopher Adams, The Death of Ivan Ilyich by Stephen Sharkey, (Attic Theatre) and Do You Love This Planet? by Alexander Matthews, Sleeping Beauty (Beacon Arts Centre), Beauty and the Beast (CAST), Aladdin (Theatr Clwyd).

LAMDA training included a placement with The Jamie Lloyd Company/ATG production of Doctor Faustus.

KAYELA BAXE – Assistant Director

Kaleya Baxe is a writer, director and facilitator who studied the BA (Hons) in Drama, Applied Theatre and Education at the Royal Central.

Theatre credits as Director include: What Makes You Feel Safe? (Guildhall School of Music and Drama); The Procurement Department (The Bunker); Her (R)age (Theatre503). Theatre credits as Assistant Director include: Boom (Theatre503); The Wonderful World of Dissocia (Arcola Theatre); The UK's Baddest Kids: The TV Show (Kiln Theatre). Theatre credits as Playwright include; Never Forget (Tristan Bates Theatre).

Kaleya is currently training on the Young Vic Intro to Directing course mentored by Roy Alexander Weise. She is also a freelance facilitator for organisations such as Tangle African & Caribbean Theatre.

PAUL CASEY – General Manager for Arden Entertainment

Paul's recent productions include Tumulus (Soho Theatre), My Name Is Rachel Corrie (Young Vic), The Night Before Christmas (Southwark Playhouse), Howard Brenton's Magnificence (Finborough Theatre) and international cabaret performer Michael Griffiths at Royal Albert Hall.

General management projects include Cafe Society Swing (Theatre Royal Stratford East), a series of new plays by Alexander Matthews (Tristan Bates Theatre), Talk Radio (Old Red Lion), All or Nothing the Mod Musical (UK Tour) and workshops for musicals of Beaches and Sugar.

In Australia, Paul was executive producer of one of Melbourne's most respected independent theatres, fortyfivedownstairs, where he produced new works in association with Melbourne International Arts Festival, Melbourne Fashion Festival and Victorian Multicultural Commission.

Paul had an extensive business management career having worked for leading fashion and retail organisations.

Radio

For Dad

Author's Note

Special thanks to Josh Roche, Abigail Gonda at Audible and Rose Cobbe at United for bringing this play back to life. *Radio* was written originally for the Kandinsky Theatre Company and staged at the 2006 Edinburgh Festival Fringe. At Kandinsky, I am hugely grateful to James Yeatman, Tom Ferguson, Oscar Mathew, Fran Bennett, Neil Hobbs and Lauren Mooney. Along the way, the writing of this play has been helped hugely by Hal Chambers and Joe Bone, Lucy Atkinson and Adam Marvel, Ben Scheuer and Eli Quetin. Thanks also to Andrew Smith and Oliver Bevan for their forensic knowledge of the Apollo era. Above all, thanks to Des and Frank, and to my Dad, Bruce Smith. In 1965, as a young physicist, he moved to Washington DC with my mother and took a job at Bell Labs where he was employed as a member of the team which selected the landing sites for the first manned Moon mission. Thanks for filling my head with ideas and giving me the freedom to have ideas of my own.

Characters

Charles L. Fairbanks Jr

All other parts to be played by the same performer.

The magnificent desolation of a Moon crater, a bomb crater, or a skate park. **Charles L. Fairbanks Jr** *sits amidst the darkness.*

Fairbanks Jr   Maybe you wanna see an effect?

A piece of magic?

You know you can tell that you aren't seeing a real magician if he calls it a trick; it's an effect in the business and I should know, say. Not that I'm in the business, I'm not in the business.

He gets nothing back. He searches his pockets.

You don't have a deck of cards on you anywhere? Everyone should keep on their person, a card or two, that's what my mother said.

He checks his pockets.

What do I got to play with . . .

He looks at his boots.

The Choker. You know about that one? That effect?

He doubles down and pulls a boot off and starts to take the lace out.

Plain old classic, the Choker, stone cold.

He gets the lace out.

So, here you put a loop in it like that and you wrap it around your throat like so and –

He tries to pull it off. It looks like he is strangling himself.

Help . . .

He goes purple.

Help!

He pulls the choker and it magically passes through his neck. He is fine.

It's just a trick, I mean an effect – there's no harm in it?

Beat.

Say I don't know how to talk to you either. Maybe you could loosen up a touch, this is as tricky for me as it is for you –

I didn't sleep well, last night. I went on quite a journey thinking about where to start. All she said was not to fill your head with shit you don't need to know.

I don't really know where my story ends and where yours begins. I don't know much about your story at all but I don't want you to feel that it's for you to say. I guess we'll have time – I hope we'll have time for that. If this goes well.

Christmas. Christmas *Eve*, '68 – that's where a whole night's thinking tells me to start. When I was seventeen. We were both seventeen. We were both up Castro Hill with a telescope. It was good and clear as I recall, and we lay out on that grass and messed around a little, before falling back and staring up into that blackness. We'd stolen a pack a' cigarettes from the El Salvadorian and said we had to tell each other something new for every drag we took.

There may have been a little else mixed in too, I don't want to encourage that but as our stories and smoke drifted up, we both said how much it felt like we were falling off the face of the Earth. And that's how it felt last night. Adrift, somewhat? Maybe you feel that too?

She went first – she told me that when we die, our souls leave our bodies and float up to the Moon. She said that the moonlight is our ancestors' way of showing us out of the darkness when we're lost.

In return, I tried to impress her. Told her that the moonlight takes three seconds to reach us, and the star that doesn't flicker – Venus – that her light takes a whole minute, and that the sunlight, that takes a whole eight minutes.

She didn't believe me. She said if the Sun took eight minutes, what would happen if it went out during that time? We'd still see it, but it wouldn't be there any more, it'd be a lie.

And so I said that of all of those other stars, their lights have been coming toward us for thousands, maybe millions of years, and that some of those lights began their journeys before the Earth was even born.

She went quiet, told me about a repeating dream she had. In her dream, she ran down Castro Hill, as fast as she could. And she got faster and faster and faster, until the light that was coming towards her got slower and slower, nearer and closer until she could touch it, and punch through it, 'Like a rock through paper', she said. And she'd keep running, faster and faster into that blackness, on and on with the Earth getting smaller and smaller behind her and the future getting nearer and closer, until she'd stop, turn around, sit back in the blackness, and wait for the past to catch up.

Lying there, drifting up into those ancient lights, was exactly like looking into the past. It is looking into the past. History, I think, is simply a property of light.

He looks at the lace in his hands.

My father's hands. I got my father's hands – what've you got?

He inspects her hands.

His hands were rough, all cut up and furrowed like a vinyl record you know. You held his hands they'd play you a tune.

He'd grown up on a farm. And on his left hand, he had this half-thumbnail – said it was from the time he slammed it shut in the train door that one time he'd been outta state – said that it'd killed the root and that it'd never grown back, and that *his* father'd said:

Charles Snr (*holding a thumb up, as if covering the Earth*) Let that crippled thumb remind you never to leave this farm, y'hear. Travelin's the business a' the past, y'hear, an' whacha can' fin' here', ya can' fin' anywhere, y'hear?

Fairbanks Jr See, his old man's old man's old man had gotten tired of another Russian winter, gotten a spot aboard a boat bound for New York, gotten sick of the East Coast and started inland, gotten sore after a couple thousand miles of walking, dropped his bags where he'd stopped and called it home. He'd dragged some fella along with 'im who knew his Bible and upon seeing all those cedar trees they settled on the name, Lebanon. They started a church, threw up a few huts together, and founded what you still got now. The town of Lebanon, Kansas. They didn't need no permission, didn't have to sign no permits, didn't have to tell no one where *they* came from.

Charles Snr   Pick a good pretty spot, read the Good Book to anyone who doesn't wancha there, and if they still don't wancha there, shoot 'em.

Fairbanks Jr   So there they were, Lebanon, and there they remained. Generation after generation, near two hundred years a' men in my family, all cutting up the land, seeding it, feeding it, cutting it up some more, all the way through to my old man.

And between every grandfather and father, every father and son, each man added a little colour to the history, some word or phrase to the great Chinese whisper. And so too did I add a little flourish with my life. Shit, it's what I heard, and who cares if it's not all true. Every story gets a little bent along the way and you'll be forgiven for that too, when it comes. So here's what I'm adding.

And if you want to know about me, you got to know how my father meets my mother.

Beat.

There'd been a dance, you see, over in the town square of Burr Oak, not five miles from Lebanon, and everyone was going.

My father, a confident man even then, hustled a couple a' his closest buddies together, and told 'em all that they were gonna go make out with all the pretty girls from Burr Oak. I remember what he said:

Charles Snr   We're gonna get ourselves the smoothest a' get-ups, shine up our hair with the slickest a' grease, think up the sharpest a' stories to get us the hottest a' girls. Now if there's one thing you never do the first time you meet a doll, you never tell her who you really are. Make up a story, they like a bit a' mystery, they'll get over the lie, so tell 'em you're a spy, or a navy diver, or a fighter pilot.

Fairbanks Jr   And in they went, buckled up to the necks in these big ol' military jackets their fathers'd all had.

Charles Snr   Even though we was sweatin' our heads off, we slung into that tent like we owned the place. Now we can't have been there five minutes before we saw a couple a' girls standing to one side. Your mother was taller than the rest . . . and I ain't a big guy, but I like a challenge. We braced ourselves and prepared our stories. And over I went. 'Hi. I'm Chuck, I'm a test pilot, fresh outta Topeka Air Force Base on furlough with my buddies right here' – the Air Force routine, always successful. 'Darlin', my life is incredibly dangerous – the planes I fly, they only got a one-in-four survival rate, and hell, I figured with those odds, I'd sure like to take my chances with you.'

Fairbanks Jr   And hell she knew it was a crock a' shit but she laughed, and thank God she did, cos she didn't you wouldn't a' got me. As a tailor's daughter she was well placed to spin him her own crock a' shit too about having just auditioned in California to become a Golden State Starlet, but I don't think he was much interested in talking.

And they danced, and they were happy, both smitten at an age not much older than when I . . . when I went up that hill and – yeah.

My father, he bought a bicycle and spent most a' his time hikin' it up and down the road to Burr Oak, day in, day out. I say *up* the road to Burr Oak but there ain't much of an *up* to anything now that I think about it. Kansas is flat as a pancake.

Flatter than a pancake, if you actually measure it, which they have, of course, from way up there, you know?

By the age of eighteen, she hopped on the back a' his bike, and together they freewheeled into holy matrimony.

Her father didn't approve of the union, mind. Not because he didn't appreciate my father in particular, more that the happy couple wouldn't let him do his schtick at their wedding.

See, he might have been a tailor in the phone book but he wasn't much of a tailor anyplace else. He had his heart set on magic; called himself the Great Dante of the Mid West. But truth be told the only thing he could make disappear with any whiff of surprise were the family savings. My mother's father was the single worst magician in the state of Kansas, I swear to God.

He'd do illusions for us all on special occasions. He spent what little money they had on effects but the doves or rabbits he used were only ever single use. Whenever you'd go eat over at their place the Thanksgiving turkey was always a Thanksgiving dove and the stuffing made from one of them rabbits that never made it out of the hat.

And while he was pursuing his dreams my mother, and I'm talking a child back then, used to keep his business on its toes.

She had an evening job taking in the orders for her father to do, but instead of waiting for him to get around to it, she'd just do them herself before the Sun came up. She could do anything. Re-line a suit while you wait, pattern cut a pair of pants overnight from little more than a cursory look. Of course she knew her new beau wasn't in the Air Force, cos all those real Air Force men got their jackets taken in and out in that store. Every pilot, past, present and future went in there at some point and my mother said she could tell the rank of a man from the weight of his jacket alone.

She was proud of her work but never spoke of it. Instead, she'd leave hidden signatures in places only she knew. She used to sew playing cards into the linings of those jackets so she could know for herself that she had a little secret on everyone.

It broke her heart to see her father pursue his dream. She'd always applauded his shows, no matter how bad they were. She didn't want to knock him by seeming unimpressed. But at the same time, she didn't want him to take her applause as a sign of encouragement.

Martha   Why don't you stay home and fix these clothes with me, Pa?

Martha's Father   Little girl, I'm doing all this for *you*!

Fairbanks Jr   That's a heavy load, for a kid. I think that's why she went for a farmer from Lebanon, when he came along. Here was a man with dirt under his nails. And there's something solid in that.

And they were happy, at least to start. It wasn't the biggest farm but he knew the business. He grew Turkey Red wheat, a grain that wasn't native to Kansas but shot up through that ground like liquorice through a goose. He still had a jar on his shelf full of the seeds that were carried across the continents by those first settlers, those Russian Mennonites.

Mother always tried to keep a parcel of land blooming with things gone by. A corner of cottonwood, a patch of Little Bluestem, not because she was anchored to the past, more she knew how to prepare for the future.

Martha   Little Bluestem's a grass been here longer than any people above the ground, Russian, native or otherwise. Little Bluestem survived the dustbowl, be around long after this breadbasket's empty.

Beat.

Fairbanks Jr   Now, it wasn't until the end of 1947 that they finally unearthed the real history of their little Lebanon. A team of men from the Geographical Survey showed up with all their maps and compasses and God knows what else to help determine wherever the hell they were and marched right up to my father's patch, knocked on the farm door a few times, and proclaimed, with all the hoopla they could carry with them that −

Cartographer   Here, right here, on this very soil, a little outside of Lebanon, Kansas, is the dead centre of the United States! Congratulations!

Fairbanks Jr   Immediately, they were put on the map.

Soon enough, the people started to arrive. Folk came from all over, took it in turns to stand at the centre, to be able to say 'I have been to the centre of the Earth, to Lebanon, to the new pole, the holy fulcrum around which this great nation spins.'

My mother says she never did hide her disapproval − she couldn't stand the visitors who started to show, their constant photographs and stupid questions:

Tourist   You live here?!

Martha   Yes.

Tourist   Gee! How does it feel to live at the centre of America?!

Martha   Feels the same as any place else.

Tourist   You must be so proud.

Martha   That's right, I'm just so proud, thrilled, and happy.

Tourist   Can I get a photograph?

Martha   No. Now, get off my Little Bluestem.

Fairbanks Jr   Soon as your place gets its name on a map, people assume it's public property and stomp all over it. Drove her up the fuckin' wall. Sorry.

She began to feel ashamed of it all − these were the fans of make-believe, the kind of folk who take pleasure in magic

shows. My father tried to keep her occupied of course, tried
to convince her there was value to be had in these visitors,
that they should make the most of it –

Charles Snr   These people are comin' from all over, from
all four corners, but this farm don't look no different from any
other farm, one mile, ten miles, a hundred miles up the road.
We gotta give them something to see!

Fairbanks Jr   I remember my father telling me that early
one morning he'd collected up all the old farm machinery
that had been put out of use, piled it all together in the front
yard for the back-hoes to scoop. My mother, she screamed
high hell –

Martha   Charles! You can't get rid of those things! It won't
last, Charles, these things never do!

Charles Snr   There's no point it sitting around, Martha,
the ground's drying up.

Martha   These things never last, Charles – throw that away,
you throw away your heart!

Beat.

Fairbanks Jr   Soon as the Sun came up, the people started
to arrive in their buses, their jaws and cameras flopping
around with the excitement of seeing what it looked like at
the centre of the world. The doors of the buses slid open, the
people spilt out into the front yard. And lo and behold, before
them stood this towering pile of junk!

Tourists   What is it?

It's a sign!

A symbol!

A monument!

To the centre!

The centre!

(Quick, take a picture.)

Fairbanks Jr   What more did they need? It had to be the centre – it had to be!

And so, the pile of crap was saved.

Of course, people wanted to touch this thing, to feel it and rub it and smell the rust on their fingers. Eventually, after people had torn strips away from the thing, people started hurting themselves, getting blood on their hands from the flecks of picked-away paint and unriveted sheets.

It all came to a head one sunny afternoon in 1948, when the fat son of the Mayor of Lebanon cut his tongue whilst licking off some ice cream he'd dripped on the thing. The town hall intervened, declared the thing dangerous, and finally sent in the tractors to drag it all away. In its place, they installed a permanent concrete pyramid fitted with a fake brass plaque that read 'The Geographical Centre of the United States'.

And with those trucks went my mother's heart. I think, of all the times she might have left him, that could have been it. But just as America found its centre in her back yard, so too did he find a bullseye in her, of a sort. Me.

And as they began setting about the necessary business of waiting those few months for my arrival, my parents slowly started to develop the skills they had tending the land into something new. She brought in a tonne of fabrics from an old supplier her father knew, and together they started making American flags with the word Lebanon alongside its facts and figures of geography. They put their heart and soul into that new business, and of course, the people loved it.

Beat.

Finding yourself in the middle of things must be a hereditary trait for us Fairbanks, cos one hot June day in 1950, my mother, reaching bursting point, lay down upon the birthing slab at Smith County Hospital, had her legs prised apart and allowed me to fall out. It was noon, June 21st 1950, the *precise* midpoint of the twentieth century – the tipping-point, if you will, at which an already troubled century reached the summit of its growth, and started to die.

And as I lay there, yackin' up goop from my untried lungs what with the midwife spanking the spirit a' life into me, the good doctor took his great cleaver and chopped the lifeline between me and my mother.

Doctor   Looks like you got a boy, Charles. Good work.

Fairbanks Jr   Out I flopped, into those big ol' hands of Charles Lebanon Fairbanks, the farmer turned flagmaker, now made senior by the arrival of his only son, Charles Lebanon Fairbanks, Jr.

Beat. He takes a bow.

Yes. My father's hands. That's my first memory. The older I get, the more like him I think I become.

He was picking something up, with his hands. *(Beat.)* Glass, something had smashed, and he stooped down to my height to pick up the shards. *(Dawning.)* It was a vacuum tube. He was replacing a vacuum tube for a radio that he'd put together. He had taken it out, he had dropped it, and it had smashed. There was this smell, a real sharp distinct smell, like gunpowder. Maybe that's why I remember it, because of the smell.

My mother come running in; she must have heard the noise …

Martha   Charlie?

Charles Snr   I broke the tube, Martha. I dropped it.

Martha   Well, don't let him touch the pieces, Charles. He'll cut his hands.

Charles Snr   I won't. Ya hear that? Don't touch the glass. Touch the glass, she kicks my ass.

Fairbanks Jr   He carried me across the room and sat me down on the worktop. I remember feeling weightless in his hands. I remember watching him walk over to the radio, pull the thing apart, and bring the thing back to life.

Beat.

I'd sit there, right there, for hours and hours, me on that worktop cutting out stars, and him stitching them into flags, all the time listening to that little machine as it pulled songs out of the air. I loved the country tunes, they always told a good story. At night he'd put the radio next to the window in my room and I'd sit and watch starlings and drift off to Glen Campbell, singing in the wire. Through that music, I could go everywhere and stay right here.

Man! I can't imagine a better time to have been a kid. Everywhere you looked, extraordinary things were happening; we'd climbed to the highest point on Earth, and made that look easy; we'd built planes that could fly so fast they'd a' passed you before you could hear 'em coming; but the most extraordinary thing . . . the thing that made me delirious with excitement was that we were seriously considering the idea that it would be possible for a human being to leave the planet. (*Incredulous.*) For a human being to go into space! There were men, sitting in rooms, drawing pictures of rockets that could squirt a man off the face of the Earth!

It was a pure dream world, and all these dreams found their way into my imagination through the radio. I mean, can you imagine a story more exciting that the birth of space travel?!

Easily my favourite radio show was *Fireball XL5*, I mean, who didn't want to be Steve Zodiac? (*The world becomes a spaceship.*) By night, the house became the Fireball. My room became the control cabin, what with my big windows looking out over the stars. My father always used to finish up after my mother, and as he'd start to climb the stairs, the floorboards creaking under him, he immediately became Commander Zero, the kind and gentle yet powerful and slightly frightening head of Space City.

Commander Zero   Charlie, I can hear you creeping around in there, get into bed . . .

Fairbanks Jr   In my room I'd be busy preparing my mission, checking that I had enough oxygen pills, and making sure Robert the Robot was fully powered up. As soon as their bedroom door clicked shut, it was time to board Fireball Junior, the landing vehicle that transported me, Steve Zodiac, down on to the surfaces of extra-planetary worlds.

I don't know where you've been but by then I must have become the most travelled boy alive. I'd been to over fifty planets, met hundreds of other life forms, saved the Earth from destruction no fewer than a thousand times and never left my house! This was the land of dreamers, and I was born right slap bang in the middle of it!

Beat.

At least I thought I was. At the age of eight, things were going pretty swell for us in Lebanon. Yeah, my father had given up on the Earth, and yes, he'd become a pretty good flagmaker even in my mother's eyes, and for the most part we all thought he'd got his head screwed on pretty tight until, over dinner on Christmas Day, 1958 . . .

Charles Snr   Martha. It's time to leave Lebanon.

Martha   What?!

Charles Snr   I've spoken to the Mayor, and I've sold him the farm.

Fairbanks Jr   My mother, she went apeshit.

Martha   Have you lost your mind, Charles?!

Charles Snr   He's given me a great price.

Martha   And where the fuck we gonna go?!

Charles Snr   I've been looking into a lovely spot in Rugby.

Martha   Rugby? Where's Rugby?

Charles Snr   North Dakota.

Beat.

Martha (*calmly*)   North Dakota.

Charles Snr   I hear it's lovely up there.

Martha (*beat*)   Charles Junior, go to your room.

Fairbanks Jr   There are only a few times in my memory that I remember my mother goin' nuts on my father, and that was one of 'em. I snuck up to my room and flipped on the radio.

I remember being surprised by what was on. It was an extended news programme. I remember exactly what was said.

Reporter   This afternoon, a little before 2:30 p.m. Eastern Standard Time, a Soyuz rocket blasted off close to the Russian border with Kazakhstan. On board, a small satellite, roughly the size of a beach ball, became the first human object in space. Sputnik.

Fairbanks Jr   As the morning came, and then '58 fell into '59, my father handed over the keys to the centre of the world to a delighted Mayor. In return, the Mayor paid him ten thousand dollars, with which my father bought a brand new Chevy Bel Air. Packing us all inside and covering us with his flags, we waved goodbye to the centre of the world and prepared for the drive north to the Dakotas.

The last thing I remember about Lebanon is sitting in the back of that car watching my father take to the concrete monument with a wrench. He'd handed me that jar of Turkey Red and told me to keep a hold of it like my whole life depended on it. I sat there watching, as he tore off that fake brass plaque and threw it in the trunk. Guess he wanted to feel like he was taking a piece of the centre with him.

When we got there, all the streets outside Rugby were covered in sticky snow. From a hundred miles up, this place must a' looked like a giant cobweb, its inhabitants stuck in the middle.

My father went to the town hall and collared the Mayor. Father explained our situation and asked to purchase a plot of land he'd seen on the way in, a few miles outside the town. The old Mayor must've thought he was a nut job for leaving the warmth of Kansas for the ice of Rugby, so he cut him a good deal out of sympathy, I guess.

I'm surprised my mother didn't leave him then, as it was almost entirely clear that he had completely lost his mind. With no farm to tend, or tourists to please, he buried himself in newspapers, and slowly began amassing an ever-growing pile of American flags.

It was only a few months later that we finally began to figure out what he was up to. One morning, over a giant stack of pancakes and waffles, I saw, upside down on the front page of the *Bismarck Tribune* the words 'America Welcomes a New Land!' It became clear that the United States had become just that little bit more united and that, for the price of a couple thousand Caribou, Alaska had just become the 49th State.

Almost as quickly as my mother realised the implication of all this, there was a knock on the door, behind which three excited gentlemen kindly informed my oh-so-surprised father that −

Cartographer   Here! Right here, on this very soil, a little outside a' Rugby, North Dakota, is the new dead centre of the United States! Congratulations!

Fairbanks Jr   We were back in business. It was like we'd never left.

My father had become a speculator of patriotism − he'd been dealt a bum hand being born in the middle of nowhere, and was trying to turn it around by selling people pieces of crap that they wouldn't a' bought elsewhere.

Of course, the new Mayor was delighted that Rugby got itself on the map, and my father wasted no time in informing him of the value that was to be had by finding yourself at the centre of the world.

Come the end of June 1959, barely six months after arriving there, my father doubled his money again, after selling off the new centre to the North Dakotan Tourist Board for twenty-five thousand dollars.

It should come as no surprise to you that we were preparing to leave again. We packed our bags, and took off, this time heading West. The news came in August of '59, at the point when we must've been passing through Montana, that Hawaii had been added as the 50th State of the Union. Almost as quickly as it had arrived, the centre of the world upped and left North Dakota, chased after our shiny red Bel Air, and whizzed out into the Pacific Ocean, where it sank to its death, about four hundred miles due west of California, never to be seen again. As always, my father remained a few steps ahead. I remember asking him –

Where are we going next?

Charles Snr   Doesn't matter.

Fairbanks Jr   But after Hawaii?

Charles Snr   There won't be any new states after Hawaii.

Fairbanks Jr   How do you know that?

Charles Snr   Simple. Do you have any idea how hard it is to lay out a flag with 51 stars?

Fairbanks Jr   We had no reason to stay in Rugby, my father said we could go wherever the hell we wanted. He knew the last move was his choice so this time he tried to move someplace she'd enjoy . . .

Charles Snr   So where was it, exactly?

Martha   What?

Charles Snr   Your audition?

Martha   What audition?

Charles Snr   To be a Golden State Starlet? When we met. Where did you go?

Martha   I didn't.

Charles Snr   You said you went to California . . .

Martha   Yeah, well, I lied.

Charles Snr   You lied?!

Martha   Yeah.

Charles Snr   I can't believe you lied.

Martha   You told me you were a test pilot.

Charles Snr   Did I?

Martha   Pull over, I need to pee.

Fairbanks Jr   In the hot summer of '59, the Fairbanks family moved a final time, this time to the city of San Francisco.

Beat.

Dad bought us a house near the top of Castro Hill. To me, this whole place was exotic – I'd been on this planet a whole nine years and I'd never really been up a hill, and San Francisco had more up 'n' down than side to side. Our street ran from top to bottom, with the white families living mostly up high, and the Latinos down the other end.

Right away, my father set about making new flags, hanging them from the branches and watching them flutter around while the dyes dried in the wind. Sometimes there were forty, fifty a' the things, flapping around on that tree. New neighbours must a' thought we really loved this country.

He started a new business, ran the whole thing outta the front yard. I helped him paint the sign – The San Francisco Flag Company – we called it.

The price of patriotism was running at an all time high. The airwaves were full of politicians, voicing their concerns about the Russians sticking a man up there first.

Politician   This time it won't just be a bleepin' beachball, but a floating platform over the edge a' which, those Reds could drop bombs.

Fairbanks Jr   A very worried President stood up on a podium down in Texas, and told the world not only were we gonna put a man into orbit, but we were gonna send him to the Moon and back by the end of the decade.

Now I didn't care for politics at all – but I was half way through being ten, and the very notion of a real *Fireball XL5* made me a little more than giddy.

I tuned into everything I could find. Turns out there's a strict selection process to becoming an astronaut and not everyone could apply. But I had a few things going for me. (*Listing it off on his fingers.*) One: all astronauts are men. Check! Two: they are always first sons. Check! Three: they are always married. *Shit.* Four: they were all in the forces somehow – test pilots mostly, in the Navy, or Air Force. If I was gonna be an astronaut I had almost all of it going for me, and so I set my mind on getting the rest. I confronted my father.

Pa, I think I need a space rocket.

Charles Snr   Oh yeah?

Fairbanks Jr   Yes. It's very important.

Charles Snr   Well, where you gonna put it?

Fairbanks Jr   In the tree. I'm planning to orbit the house from the tree.

Charles Snr   Of course, how stupid of me.

Fairbanks Jr   But we gotta work quick, or the Reds'll beat us to it. I'm ready to go, just need a spaceship.

Charles Snr   Well hold-up, buckaroo, surely you're gonna need a space suit?

Fairbanks Jr   Shucks! I hadn't thought a' that.

Charles Snr   Can't go into space without a space suit, buddy, it's very dangerous.

Fairbanks Jr   Of course he was right. I had seriously underestimated the dangers of orbital space-travel.

Charles Snr   But I just so happen to know the best space suit manufacturer in all of America. I'll be sure put in a good word for you.

Fairbanks Jr   And so, whilst my father started hacking into that tree, my mother began taking measurements and making me my first flight suit, mainly out of old waxed cotton and tin foil. It took us quite some time to get that thing ready for action – I helped my father get all the wood together, punch all the right kinds a' hole in the belly of the tree, and, come the spring of 1961, the craft seemed just about ready to fly, and we prepared to launch.

The heavens came down that night. Come the mornin', it was the clearest I remember, the kinda clear you only get by the ocean. I remember comin' downstairs – it was the morning of April 13th 1961, and on the front of the paper what did I find but a big old picture of some Red wazzo hangin' his heiny out up there. Beat me to it!

Our goal had to change from being the first humans in space to being the first Americans – but most people didn't know the difference so I figured that was just as good.

I completed my final checks, I made my way up the ladder and into the capsule. I looked back, I waved goodbye to my family, and I shut the door.

Five hundred million people tuned in to watch. Those close
enough stood on the ground and watched with their bare eyes,
the fires pounding their chests. Those further afield tuned in
on their radios and televisions as it was broadcast live across
every network. They watched me float around the planet,
twice, three, four times. At night, they turned their lights on
so I could make out the cities a hundred miles beneath.

I stayed there for hours, just sat there, looking out over it all,
describing what I was seeing. Out of the small window, I saw
a new dawn every ninety minutes. It was dark, it was warm,
it was perfect.

Beat.

But what goes up . . .

I was in the grocery store at the bottom of the hill when
I heard it. My mother had developed an obsession with the
First Lady and wanted the copy of *Life* magazine she was
gracing. She'd asked me to pick it up and the ingredients for
spicing a Christmas ham. I remember going into the store,
flopping the magazine on the counter, pointing at the picture
and saying:

My mother wants to look like this.

The clerk, the El Salvadorian, he didn't look at me so good.
Now, you gotta remember I knew the guy, I'd been into that
store maybe a hundred times, and every time he smiled and
showed me his gold tooth.

He had his radio on.

There was a man talking.

There had been a shooting.

A man had been shot.

He had been in his motorcade.

Crowds had been waving.

Someone heard the crack.

The man was hit.

He fell to his side.

She scrambled for the pieces.

But shooting a man doesn't snuff out the dreams he builds, it just slows 'em down.

Dreams, you see, aren't weightless things. They have a mass, as small as you like, but a mass nonetheless. And when you gather such a great collection of those tiny weights, as you had when everyone dreamed the same thing, those weights built up one hell of a swing, enough to sling us all round the Moon and back. He put that weight in all of us.

I sure as hell carried mine. In '63, I'd just turned thirteen, was growing a rate about a foot a week and everything hurt. Thirteen's a difficult year, was for me and for the country both. I guess the President's death shoved us into the real world for the first time.

Beat.

At about the same time, my father gave me my first job. He picked up an old bicycle, fixed a basket on the front, filled the thing with flags and handed me a scrap of paper with all these addresses on it. Wheeling me to the edge of the driveway, he gave me a push on the back and watched as I started rolling away. I hadn't even reached the end of the block before gravity got the better of me.

After a hundred yards or so, I was going just about as fast as I'd ever been in a car, my father chasing after me down the hill. I could see the freeway interchange at the bottom was getting almighty close. My hands started to shake like hell, I did a little thinkin' and I figured it was either get mushed by a truck or spill off into some yard and hope for the best. I closed my eyes, yanked the handlebars across, ripped through

a hedge, slammed into a porch and was launched, along with
the contents of my basket, through her bedroom window.

My flight came to a stop pretty much at her feet. I got up
brushed the dust and glass off my coat, pulled the flag off of
my head and said:

Hi. I'm Captain America.

I think I must've passed out right after that, as the next thing
I remember was sitting outside that house with a cup of
lemonade and my father promising to pay her father for the
broken window. I'd busted my arm up pretty bad, and she was
sitting next to me with a bowl a' warm water cleaning me up.

She said she'd never met a boy who could fly before.

I never told her I couldn't. In fact, I think maybe I still can.

Her father wouldn't accept money for the window – he was
laughing too hard. He did accept the offer for dinner though.

I still remember the look on my mother's face when her two
boys came home for dinner, followed by an entire Mexican
family? That's somethin' you never forget.

Over dinner, her father told my father all about his politics –
kept goin' on and on about the neglected Latino contribution
to the great state of California. In the kitchen, my mother was
busy givin' his wife a detailed instruction on how to bake the
perfect Christmas ham. It all got a little heated, and I don't
think they even noticed that she'd taken my hand and led me
into the garden.

She and I stood before that tree. The Moon was hanging in its
branches. She looked up to my spacecraft and asked whether
she could get inside. Space is only for boys, I said!

She looked at me like I was the stupidest asshole on the face
of the planet, grabbed me by the hand, and laid one right on
me, right on the lips.

Immediately, space became a free-for-all – and, please, ladies first.

From inside, we could see the whole of the bay, from Oakland to Alcatraz, with the Moon sitting next to us, picking it all out like a giant spotlight.

I told her I was gonna go to the Moon some day. She smiled and asked me to send her a postcard. She didn't doubt me for a second, and right then I think the Moon got a little closer. I was a man, I was a first son, and I swear I could have married her.

We stayed there until our fathers staggered out to collect us. They were both drunk and laughin' about a plan they'd hatched to start makin' flags together.

What my father had in ambition, her father matched in business smarts. He'd trained as an accountant in Mexico and was now working as a janitor over the bay in Berkeley. He said the students up there were burning flags the whole time. In fact, they couldn't get hands on the Stars and Stripes fast enough. He told my father he could save a fortune if he used a cheaper material, especially as they were only going up in smoke after a single use. Of course my father jumped at the idea. In addition to her father sayin' he could get hold of a couple dozen Mexican fellas who'd happily put their weight behind such a good cause, they helped each other out in setting up a stall on the campus. Demand was so high, they even started weaving magnesium into the fabric so those flags'd burn brighter and faster.

Come the beginning of '65, they'd set up outlet stores at every college on the West Coast. Cal, UCSB, the new place in La Jolla, they were all stuffed rigid with kids pursuing degrees less in the liberal arts and more in liberal arson. Now that the business had someone with a head for numbers, the San Francisco Flag Company was fast becoming the most prominent distributor of all things American this side of the Rockies. And come the summer of '66, my father couldn't believe his luck when Vietnam properly kicked off – so many Americans were dyin' out there that the demand for American flags at military funerals went through the roof.

Pride and protest, he used to laugh, they're lucrative things.

Beat. He shakes his head, uncomfortable with that.

Over the next eighteen months, they set up distribution points for the San Francisco Flag Company in every state. The worse it got, the better it got. For them, at least.

Beat.

September 2nd 1968. My mother was standing in the driveway when I came home. She had been crying. In one hand she held the pair of socks she was darning. And in the other an unopened envelope.

The United States Draft Board had deemed that the fairest way to select young men to go fight was to pull random birthdays and area codes out a' hat. She didn't have to open it to know I'd be back at the centre of things. It's the family way, I guess.

My mother screamed blue murder as the draft bus pulled up.

Martha   I'm sorry sir, you got this wrong.

Fairbanks Jr   I tried to stop her –

Martha   There's a doctor's report if you have another look –

Fairbanks Jr   Mom –

Martha   He's still growing and it's a physiological condition that makes him unfit to fight – check the draft number again, it ain't A1, I'll tell you that.

Fairbanks Jr   Mom, it's OK –

Martha   There's a doctor's report –

Fairbanks Jr   It doesn't matter –

Martha   But we paid for it already –

Fairbanks Jr   I want to go –

Martha   We made a contribution

Fairbanks Jr   I signed up, Mom. This ain't the draft –

Martha   You signed up.

Fairbanks Jr   Yeah.

Martha   Why?

Fairbanks Jr   I'm gonna be an astronaut. This is how it's done.

And there it was.

Martha   Why don't you stay home and fix these clothes with me, huh?

Fairbanks Jr   I got on the bus to do my basic. Eight weeks down the coast at Fort Ord. My folks barely recognised me the weekend we got to say our goodbyes. I'd lost all the hair on my head and twenty-five pounds round the waist. Those pants were hanging off me but my mother said nothing.

Dad and I. We talked about everything but the obvious. He didn't seem so keen to talk about flags for caskets now and instead bragged about the contract he'd just signed to supply the flags for the very Moon itself. Don't know which was worse to hear. He sent me off with that jar of Turkey Red and wished me luck. My mother didn't say a word.

That Saturday night, I took my girl to the top of Castro Hill. I told her why the stars flicker and she told me how our souls go to the Moon. That night, three men boarded Apollo 8 and became the first humans to break free of the Earth. As they fell into the Moon's open arms, for the first time, I knew how it could feel to let go of yourself, to separate yourself from all you thought you knew, and take on the hopes and fears of another. We held our breath as we floated through the radio silence and became the first humans to lose sight of the Earth.

In the morning, as the Earth rose out of the darkness, I knew I'd been born again.

Beat.

You get no real sense of it from all this distance – on the way up you're told there are valleys entirely untouched by white men's feet and mountains so high they're known only to the souls of the ancestors who've passed up that way in death. And from here, now, maybe all that sounds beautiful and before I went that's certainly how it seemed to me. But when you get there . . . it's . . . unspeakably hostile. There's no relief. Anywhere.

And that's not to say it's not beautiful when you're there – it is, but that beauty's so dangerous up close. When the Sun's out it's hot enough to make your blood boil and when it's hidden you'd best to get back inside lest you freeze solid.

And the view? My God it's clear. Like there's nothing between you and the horizon, like you could reach out and touch the furthest peaks without any effort at all. But that's a lie. You try to take even one breath outside of the boundaries you've been set and the air'll get ripped straight out of your lungs. It might seem friendly but the only air of home you got is what's inside your helmet. You learn not to trust your eyes.

The other boys who've been up there too'll say it the same; you're never who you were when you come back. They say that to stand in those craters, to be able to look up and cover the Earth with your thumb – that that does something to you. A spiritual damage. They have a name for it – Detachment Syndrome. They say that once you've seen the things that I've seen, once you'd done the things that I've done, you can never describe that experience to someone else. A part of you never comes back.

Beat.

On July 21st, we all went outside. We switched on our radio, stood in those colourless craters and looked up. It was night time for us, everything was black and white.

I knew my Old Man was watching. He'd written me, said he'd supplied the flag we'd plant and that into its stars he'd sewn my name.

Charles Snr   You're on the Moon now, kid. From what they say you'll be there forever.

Beat.

Fairbanks Jr   There weren't many words carried up from home. It's all business on the Squawk Box, chatter between base and all the other men scattered across the desolation.

I wrote my father back, time and again, and asked him if he'd be sending up the flags on all the rockets to come –

'Say, Apollo 12 got struck by lightning on launch, huh, how about that?! And how about 13, Dad! You see the job those boys did in that tin can?! Houston! We got a problem!'

I wrote but nothing came back. My girl didn't write me back neither. I sent her postcards like she asked, but nothing ever got returned. Suppose out of sight, out of mind, and three years is a long time when you're seventeen. The guys would ask me about her, poke me for a picture. But I didn't have one. Think they thought I was full of shit. That I was just saying I had a girl to fit in.

I stopped talking about her after a while, I didn't like their jokes. I kept her clear in my head, mind, retold myself the story of us, over and over. But everything slips when it's not said aloud and after enough silence had collected I started to wonder if I'd just made the whole thing up. If I couldn't trust my eyes maybe I couldn't trust my mind, neither.

I did get a letter, eventually. From my mom, of all people, stamped July 26th 1971.

Martha   Charles.

Your father died.

He came off the road in that damned car around Salinas.

There was some other woman in the wreckage, I don't know the whole story.

Sorry to break this to you in writing. I'm sure that it's painful, but you should know.

Your mother, Martha.

Silence.

Fairbanks Jr   Gone. Cold. The facts. No sense of shape, nothing to take the edge off, just . . . six lines and a stamp. Guess storytelling's not in her bones.

Beat.

The boys were understanding. Stopped making jokes about the girl and gave me quarters in a better crater. I tried to tell them his story but I didn't feel they deserved it. But I felt if I didn't say it to someone, anyone, it'd get lost. I don't know why I did this, honest to God, I don't know why, but I picked up the VHF, picked a channel out of range, and just started speaking. His story. As best I could remember.

I often think about that radio broadcast. My message, written on the edge of a bubble expanding in every direction at the speed of light. His whole recorded history transported on waves of light.

I don't know why I did that. An apology maybe? To Dad? To Mom, on his behalf?

Without Dad in the story things really started to twist.

Back home, 'free love' was racing its way through the mind of every dropout in America as fast as the VD through their smalls. If you weren't drafted you were a drifter and if you were lucky enough to be the latter you couldn't a' done much better for us boys than keeping your mouth shut about your freedom. But no. There they were all over the airwaves, those lucky assholes dropping their peace signs as often as their pants.

And sure standards may have been slipping back home but you'd never have expected it on the Moon. *First men and married*, them's the rules. I could just about accept that Stuart Roosa was the youngest of two brothers when he climbed aboard Apollo 14, but nothing came close to the betrayal I felt when I heard about Alfred Worden getting his seat on Apollo 15. Alfred Worden! A divorcee. In space. Jesus. Before you know it they'll be sending a woman.

Things got sloppy. The men started questioning the point of the mission −

Soldier   They're not interested in what we're doing out here, we're all the way out here for show.

Fairbanks Jr   Don't forget what that flag on your shoulder means, it shows the world what America stands for.

Soldier   Look who's drunk the Kool Aid, what a space cadet.

Fairbanks Jr   You'd better shut your mouth before you the Commander hears.

Soldier   The Cap doesn't give a fuck, shit he's saying it himself.

Fairbanks Jr   I liked the Captain, I didn't like their slurs so I went to him to straighten it out, but −

Captain   Course it's for show. We can't do shit up here. Get your head out of the clouds, Fairbanks, and try to survive till you get your ride home.

Fairbanks Jr   Detachment Syndrome. Everything you thought you stood for can be covered up with a thumb. And it ain't worth shit.

Re-entry was hard.

I'd followed Apollo 16 closely − well, as closely as I could given what few scraps I could find about it on the radio.

Apollo 17 followed with even less hoopla. I had its launch in my ears as the Hueys dropped and drowned out the countdown.

We took off at about the same time as the boys up there left the Moon's gravity, and landed on the West Coast just as they splashed down in the Pacific. Twenty after fourteen hundred hours, December 19th 1972. Their splashdown wasn't even covered, just as our returning went unnoticed. We might have gone out aboard a Freedom Bird to the fanfares of Pershing's Own but we returned to the sound of silence on a commercial 727, us shattered boys mixed in with those home for holidays. Merry Christmas, everyone.

I lost all my stuff at baggage reclaim. Some other Joe must'a taken it as his own, guess all them sacks looked the same. Still stood in line for an answer though. Two fellas at a service desk geared up to help holidaymakers repatriate their lost shit. One of them had his TV on. Kept smackin' the side, thinkin' he'd got his dial bust.

Service Clerk   Yo, you got the time, Ral'? Yo, Ral –

I chipped in.

Fairbanks Jr   Sixteen hundred, sir.

Service Clerk   Sixteen hundred.

Fairbanks Jr   Sir. Maybe five after.

Service Clerk   Then what's this crap?

Fairbanks Jr   That's Seventeen coming back.

Service Clerk   Seventeen what?

Fairbanks Jr   Apollo Seventeen.

Service Clerk   Shit, they're still going to the Moon?!

Fairbanks Jr   Sure are.

Service Clerk   Why?

Fairbanks Jr   Whaddaya mean, why?

Service Clerk   That shit's boring. Looks just the same as the last one.

Fairbanks Jr   They're up at the Poles now –

Service Clerk   They cut into *I Love Lucy* for this? Where's *I Love Lucy*. Yo, Ral, call the station, get 'em to put *Lucy* back on. Assholes.

Fairbanks Jr   It wasn't Congress that killed the space programme. It was ad revenue on CBS. I never did find my bag. All I had left were the clothes on my back and what I carried on by hand. A photograph of Dad and that old jar of Turkey Red.

I stood at the arrivals gate and waited. Dunno what for. One of the boys, as he was saying so long, asked me who I was waiting for?

Carter   Someone comin' for ya?

Fairbanks Jr   Don't think so.

Carter   Well, you want a ride? Where's home?

Fairbanks Jr   I don't know.

Carter   Well, where are your people from?

Fairbanks Jr   Lebanon?

Carter   Lebanon, Oregon!?

Fairbanks Jr   Lebanon, Kansas. It's the centre of the world.

Carter   You're in Los Angeles.

Fairbanks Jr   Sure.

Carter   Well you wanna stay at ours til you find your feet?

Fairbanks Jr   OK.

He had family just over the other side of the freeway in Lakewood. He hooked me up with a camp bed in the garage, let me use the restroom and stuff. It was nice, if a little square. The town, not the bathroom. And I really mean *square*.

Lakewood's entirely built of straight lines, not a curve to be seen. Every block is perfect.

Whole place had been built around the aircraft factory. Used to be that every young man who worked there got his own home for him and his family and my friend and his dad were no different.

Carter   Fairbanks, you out looking for work?

Fairbanks Jr   I guess.

Carter   Well what do you do all day?

Fairbanks Jr   Just sit around. Shopping malls, mostly.

Carter   You got anything else to wear?

Fairbanks Jr   Why?

Carter   Fix yourself up and I'll put in a good word.

Fairbanks Jr   I never had a job interview before. That was kind of exciting. I'd lost my uniform at the airport so I went down the thrift store and picked up the closest thing I could find. I'm sorry about the jacket. I'm not a general but it's the only thing they had in my size.

Interviewer   Mr Charles Fairbanks.

Fairbanks Jr   Jr, please. Mr Charles Fairbanks was my father, but we got the same name.

Interviewer   Why is it you'd like to work for Douglas Aircraft?

Fairbanks Jr   Well, that's an easy one. I'm gonna be an astronaut.

Interviewer   An astronaut?

Fairbanks Jr   Yes, sir. Do you have any openings for test pilots? Entry level but I'm a quick learner.

They did thank me for my service, which always helps. I didn't stay in the garage for long. I got along with Carter just fine, but his brother had some unpleasant views –

Brother   It's fake.

Fairbanks Jr   What is?

Brother   The Moon. It's a hoax. Never happened.

Fairbanks Jr   Now hold on –

Brother   Whole thing's a big sideshow the Government staged to distract us from all the kids you guys were killing over there.

Fairbanks Jr   Unbelievable. It's one thing calling me a child killer, but to say *that* . . .

I drifted for a time. The tabs of a general and the Turkey Red under my arm. Thought maybe if I could find myself a little open land and plant myself a crop I could reach back and shake the hand of my forefathers. I tried it for a while, found a little strip of green over there under the 605, turned the soil and dished it out, waited for the first shoots of spring. I may not have had a roof over my head but the good thing about Southern California is it never rains. That said, the bad thing about Southern California is it never rains and that ain't all that helpful when you're trying to get into the farming business. I tried again the next year, and the next, but nothing never took, and after a while I found myself with only a handful of the past left. I can't spill that now, can I? Else, what am I gonna pass on?

He shakes his tin.

You find there's a home to be made wherever you go, no matter how little you have. I got myself some new wheels, a Wal Mart Bel Air, and a radio of my own. I found myself new craters to live in too, 'cept these ones are used for skateboards not safety. I've got a community round here; the Alpha Dogs and Zephyr Boys call me the Radio Man. I tell them stories, keep an ear tuned in case I catch a bubble of the past to pass on. Say they learn a thing or two from an old boy like me.

'Son, American Dream's not fuelled by your own ambitions but by other people's tragedies.'

Martha   Charles?

Fairbanks Jr   'Son, if Uncle Sam gives you the heavens to enjoy take a look at what he's hiding behind his back.'

Martha   Charles?

Fairbanks Jr   'Son, we spent twenty-five billion dollars getting there only to dump six moon buggies and a half-dozen golfballs. Junk and jingo, man, they're thriftless things.'

Martha   Are you my Charlie?

Fairbanks Jr   I hadn't been called Charlie in a while.

Mom.

Martha   I didn't know you were back.

Fairbanks Jr   I didn't know you were looking.

Martha   Of course I was.

Fairbanks Jr   She said she'd only discovered I'd returned after my missing bag turned up at her door. After it lay unclaimed for long enough, someone at the airport had gone through it, found Dad's letter and reached out from there. Said she'd found Carter, said she'd heard word of a Radio Man –

I'm starting a crop, Mom! It's Turkey Red!

Martha   Why didn't you tell me?

Fairbanks Jr   Well, it hasn't grown yet, so –

Martha   That you were back.

Fairbanks Jr   You didn't write me.

Martha   I didn't like that you'd gone.

Fairbanks Jr   He deserved more than six lines.

She had been living up there, all that time, not in the same house on Castro Hill but still in San Francisco. They had to downsize, she said, seemed odd to me that they might.

Before he died, my father and the janitor had gone their separate ways. Not by choice, she said. Uncle Sam, it seems, doesn't always like the self-made man. In fact he comes looking to fill you full of holes if your money's made by un-American means. You can be a fraud and cheat, not pay your taxes or your workers and he'll turn a blind eye, but make a buck burning one flag . . .

And they really poke around. They went through the whole business, found out one of its founding fathers was in the country without papers. Must've thought they struck gold. Father played it down, course – said they'd got it all wrong –

Charles Snr   This guy? He don't own half the business, shit he's just my janitor.

Fairbanks Jr   Guess that must've really stung. The janitor might have only swept the halls at Berkeley but he swept the floor with Father when it came to numbers. I guess when you've got your head in the stars you never read the bottom line. Father found out the hard way he didn't own as much of the business as he thought, and after the janitor went south with his family so too did the business. The US Government, in its infinite wisdom, deported the nation's largest provider of American flags to Mexico. Outsourcing at its finest.

Mom tried to set me up with a job at the factory. The business had supplied a lot of the flags for the caskets coming back and she had some strings to pull with the Air Force. She tried her best but nobody's much interested in a hobo who's fallen off the face of the earth.

She set me up in a small apartment, gave me an address whilst she shuttled back and forth to San Francisco, and eventually one of her old friends came good with a temporary job in the factory kitchens, washing plates and serving up food for an event they had coming up.

Martha   You can't expect the Moon all at once, Charles. Work your way up.

Fairbanks Jr   It wasn't solid work but it was good work when it came. Satisfyingly invisible. Every now and then I'd get called in, some banquet or gala for which they needed extra staff.

I wanted to thank Mom, to get to know her better, but she had her hands full with her own business up north – said she was raising a patch of Little Bluestem. I told her:

Nothing grows out here, Mom –

But she persisted. We'd speak now and then and I'd invite her down to stay but she said I should work on getting myself more established before I thought about visitors. Made it seem like she didn't like to impose. Huh.

But that all changed when Gerald Ford came to town. He was due to pay a visit along with the head of the US Air Force; the latter showing the former around where their beloved bombers were born.

I called Mom –

Mom, I don't have the money to thank you for helping me but how d'you feel about meeting the President and the First Lady?

Mrs Ford was no Jackie O, but Mother was down before I'd hung up the phone.

It was an elegant affair. I'd been promoted to the floor team and guests would have the privilege of eating my canapés under the wings of those angels of death. I got Mom a ticket. She wore her best dress. Gave me a lot of pride to see her there.

They'd hired a magician. Some hotshot Hollywood showboater with impossible teeth.

He had good shtick, a clean patter you know. If he was shitting himself for the President you couldn't tell. He needed an assistant for his final effect. Here and there, a few folk put their hands up, businessmen pushing forward their giggling dates, their big hands on their asses. After a joke or two about promising to return them in one piece he picked one – a woman right in his eyeline.

Now I hadn't paid much attention till this point – I was working my way through the vol-au-vents while everyone's backs were turned – but the woman he picked was my mother. Up she went and took to his side.

I don't remember what he needed her help for, pulling something or other out of a hat. But it went well, and people laughed and oohed and aahed as he needed. But just as the crowd had finished clapping, my mother steps up and asks: 'Can I do a trick?'

The whole hangar falls silent. The magician laughs, nervous. What did she just say?

Martha   Can I do a trick? An effect? For the President?

Fairbanks Jr   The magician tries to laugh it off and move on, but the President pipes up –

Ford   Say, if woman wants to show herself up let's see it.

Fairbanks Jr   So there's my mother, the stage her own by Presidential decree.

Martha   You got a pack of cards there, sport?

Fairbanks Jr   The room laughs.

Magician   Well, not on me.

Martha   Everyone should keep on their person a card or two, especially a magician.

He pulls out a deck of cards from a pocket.

Fairbanks Jr   The room laughs more. My mother whips the plastic off like it's a new pack of smokes. She takes the deck, shuffles it like a seasoned croupier which gets a few people whispering before she fixes the President's Wife and asks –

Martha   Mrs Ford, why don't you come on up here and pick a card.

Fairbanks Jr   More silence. The President laughs.

Ford   Well go on then, you heard the lady.

Fairbanks Jr   Up walks Mrs Ford. Picks a card from the deck fanned out in my mother's unshaking hands.

Martha   Got it?

Mrs Ford   Sure.

Martha   Well, you remember that card, then put it back in the deck anywhere you like and give it a good shuffle.

Fairbanks Jr   Mrs Ford shuffles the deck. The magician over here starts laughing too, like he's cool with all this but he ain't cool.

Martha   Satisfied, that that pack's fully shuffled?

Mrs Ford   Yes, ma'am.

Fairbanks Jr   Mother takes back the deck. Holds it behind her back and pulls out a card.

Martha   Your card, Mrs Ford, was the ten of clubs.

Mrs Ford   No, no it wasn't.

Fairbanks Jr   The magician stops laughing.

Martha   Are you *sure*, Mrs Ford?

Beat.

Mrs Ford   I'm sure of it. It wasn't the ten of clubs.

Martha   But are you *really* sure?

Fairbanks Jr   The magician steps forward. My mother's really screwing up his act.

Magician   Hey, maybe that's –

Fairbanks Jr   My mother stops him with the kind of look that tenderises meat.

Martha   Then what was it? What card did you pick, Mrs Ford?

Mrs Ford   The ace of hearts.

Fairbanks Jr   Huh. My mum plays it like she's bummed out, like she's fucked up, and holds it for a second before turning to the President himself and asks, cool as you like –

Martha   Mr President, what'd you give me if I told you your wife's card's inside the lining of your friend here's jacket?

Fairbanks Jr   She points at David C. Jones, his host.

The President laughs.

Ford   My friend's jacket?

Martha   Yeah. Your friend there. Chief of the Air Staff.

Ford   Well, shit, I think I'd give you just about anything you asked for.

Martha   Go on then. Take your steak knife right there and cut him open. Left side, breast pocket.

Fairbanks Jr   The room holds its breath as President Gerald Ford starts cutting into the jacket of the Chief of the US Air Force. My mother looks at me. The penny drops, just as the President reaches into the general's coat and pulls out . . .

Ford   The ace of hearts.

Fairbanks Jr   The room goes nuts. The magician's out of business and there's a new star in town.

Ford   How did you do that, young lady?

Martha   A magician never tells. But you said I could have anything I wanted.

Ford   And what do you want?

Martha   Give my son a job. A permanent placement. He's the serviceman at the back eating all the canapés cos he can't afford his dinner.

Fairbanks Jr   I met the President of the United States that night. He asked me what kind of job I wanted and of all the people who could actually have realised my dream I sincerely forgot to ask him whether I could be an astronaut.

I took Mom out right after. We went to a bar on Bellflower and I'm telling you, that woman can drink. I told her I couldn't believe what she'd done.

Martha   Why not?

Fairbanks Jr   Didn't know you had that in you.

Martha   No?

Fairbanks Jr   Well, you never showed me any tricks before.

Martha   You didn't ask.

Fairbanks Jr   I never knew.

Martha   Then growing up maybe you should've made a little space for your mother's story, huh? Another whisky.

Fairbanks Jr   Mom stuck around the next day. Helped me clear up the spare room.

I don't need all this space, Mom. It's too big.

Martha   Now that you got your permanent fix you need a little space for Little Bluestem.

Fairbanks Jr   I tried growing things out here, Mom. You can forget about your flowers . . .

Martha   Little Blue's not a flower, Charlie. She's a little girl, and she's yours.

Beat.

Fairbanks Jr   She never called me Charlie.

Martha   She's a little girl, and she's yours. Are you hearing me?

Fairbanks Jr   Little Bluestem?

Martha   Yeah. Blue, for short. (*Beat.*) Rosa had to go back to Mexico with her parents. But Little Blue's still there with me.

Fairbanks Jr   In San Francisco?

Martha   Why d'you think I keep going north?

Fairbanks Jr   I've got a daughter named Little Blue?!

Martha   Uh-uh. So you'd better get the room fixed cos she's coming down tomorrow. Work out what you're gonna say to her and don't fill her head with shit she doesn't need to know.

A new dawn.

Fairbanks Jr   I . . . I read that . . . one of the guys on Apollo 12 had his mind blown open so wide by walking on the Moon that he couldn't just come back and return to who he was. Said he'd sit around in shopping malls, just watching people walk around, thinking to himself that he'd been to a place where all of them and everyone who's ever been since the dawn of time could be covered up behind his thumb. Someone asked him if that made him feel empty and he said quite the opposite – it made him realise how special we are. That in this universe we've only got each other and that the real achievement for Apollo wasn't that we got there but that in getting there we realised the value of all we'd left behind.

The way I see you, I know how he feels. Sometimes even I go and sit in a mall hoping someone else might mistake me for the right kind of fallen hero but I doubt he got *his* clothes at a thrift store.

Beat.

There's no way to dodge the horrors of it all. Just try not to get lost behind your own thumb. Guess that's all I can offer.

Unless, maybe you wanna see an effect? A piece of magic? You know you can tell that you aren't seeing a real magician if he calls it a trick; it's an effect in the business and I should know, say. Not that I'm in the business.

I'm not in the business.

Blackout.

Methuen Drama Modern Plays

include work by

Bola Agbaje
Edward Albee
Davey Anderson
Jean Anouilh
John Arden
Peter Barnes
Sebastian Barry
Alistair Beaton
Brendan Behan
Edward Bond
William Boyd
Bertolt Brecht
Howard Brenton
Amelia Bullmore
Anthony Burgess
Leo Butler
Jim Cartwright
Lolita Chakrabarti
Caryl Churchill
Lucinda Coxon
Curious Directive
Nick Darke
Shelagh Delaney
Ishy Din
Claire Dowie
David Edgar
David Eldridge
Dario Fo
Michael Frayn
John Godber
Paul Godfrey
James Graham
David Greig
John Guare
Mark Haddon
Peter Handke
David Harrower
Jonathan Harvey
Iain Heggie

Robert Holman
Caroline Horton
Terry Johnson
Sarah Kane
Barrie Keeffe
Doug Lucie
Anders Lustgarten
David Mamet
Patrick Marber
Martin McDonagh
Arthur Miller
D. C. Moore
Tom Murphy
Phyllis Nagy
Anthony Neilson
Peter Nichols
Joe Orton
Joe Penhall
Luigi Pirandello
Stephen Poliakoff
Lucy Prebble
Peter Quilter
Mark Ravenhill
Philip Ridley
Willy Russell
Jean-Paul Sartre
Sam Shepard
Martin Sherman
Wole Soyinka
Simon Stephens
Peter Straughan
Kate Tempest
Theatre Workshop
Judy Upton
Timberlake Wertenbaker
Roy Williams
Snoo Wilson
Frances Ya-Chu Cowhig
Benjamin Zephaniah

For a complete listing of
Methuen Drama titles, visit:

www.bloomsbury.com/drama

Follow us on Twitter and keep up to date
with our news and publications

@MethuenDrama